Heaven-Sent

Love Letters

Between Tom in Heaven and
Nancy on Earth

Nancy S. Calumet

Nancy

"Message in a Bottle", drawing by Maddie McAllister

Between Tom in Heaven and Nancy on Earth

By Nancy S. Calumet

This astonishing collection of real letters, between a widow on Earth and her deceased husband in Heaven, will amaze, thrill, and encourage you as to possibilities of the life to come.

Cover art by Maddie McAllister
Other art by Marcia McMahon and James Murray
Clip art by Creative Commons, powered by Bing
Photographs by Sister Mary Ellen, pp. 6 and 63

Nancy's Flowers
Original watercolor by Marcia McMahon
www.marymagdalenesmessage.com

© Copyright 2021 N. S. Calumet

ISBN 13: 978-1-62329-069-6
ISBN 10: 1-62329-069-4

Mercer Publications & Ministries, Inc., Publisher 2021
Stanwood, Michigan USA

Copying is prohibited without the consent of the author, except for brief quotes in literary reviews or commentaries.

Dedication

Dedicated

To my husband
Thomas Anthony Calumet
(May 14, 1927—February 2, 1990)

To my brother
James Clarence Spresser, Ph.D.
(May 16, 1947—April 3, 2020)

To all people who have lost a loved one.

To our angels who inspire us, bringing us closer together.

"To be loved for what one is, that is the greatest exception. The great majority love in others only what they lend him, their own selves, their version of him."

"This is the true measure of love:
When we believe that we alone can love,
That no one could ever have loved so before us,
And that no one will ever love in the same way after us."

— Johann Wolfgang von Goethe

CONTENTS

Dedication _____ *vii*

Acknowledgements _____ *xii*

Introduction by Nancy S. Calumet _____ *xiii*

Introduction by Thomas Anthony Calumet _____ *xviii*

Foreword by James Murray _____ *1*

September 30, 2017 _____ *2*

October 20, 2017 _____ *3*

October 20, 2017 _____ *7*

March 20, 2018 _____ *3*

March 24, 2018 _____ *8*

April 11, 2018 _____ *9*

April 11, 2018 _____ *10*

April 14, 2018 _____ *11*

May 14, 2018 _____ *12*

May 20, 2018 _____ *13*

May 27, 2018 _____ *15*

June 26, 2018 _____ *16*

June 26, 2018 _____ *17*

July 25, 2018 _____ *18*

July 26, 2018 _____ *19*

August 30, 2018 _____ *20*

September 5, 2018 _____ *22*

September 13 2018 _____ *23*

September 15, 2018	24
September 18, 2018	25
September 20. 2018	26
October 2, 2018	27
Tom's October Letter to Nancy	28
October 8, 2018	31
October 12, 2018	32
October 20, 2018	33
November 1, 2018	34
Tom's November Letter	35
November 17, 2018	37
November 24, 2018	39
December 14, 2018	40
January 2019	42
January 10, 2019	44
January 13, 2019	46
January 20, 2019	47
January 22, 2019	50
February 14, 2019	53
February 17, 2019	54
February 28, 2019	55
March 4, 2019	56
March 15, 2019	57
March 20, 2019	59
March 31, 2019	61

March 31, 2019	62
April 2, 2019	64
April 10, 2019	66
April 16, 2019	67
April 22, 2019	69
May 2 2019	71
May 10, 2020	73
May 17, 2019	75
May 30, 2019	77
June 12, 2019	80
June 28. 2019	82
July 4, 2019	84
End Notes	86
Final Chapter	88
About the Author	91
INDEX OF WORKS OF ART	92

Acknowledgements

Thank you, my friends, for tirelessly aiding me along the way in the completion of this book:

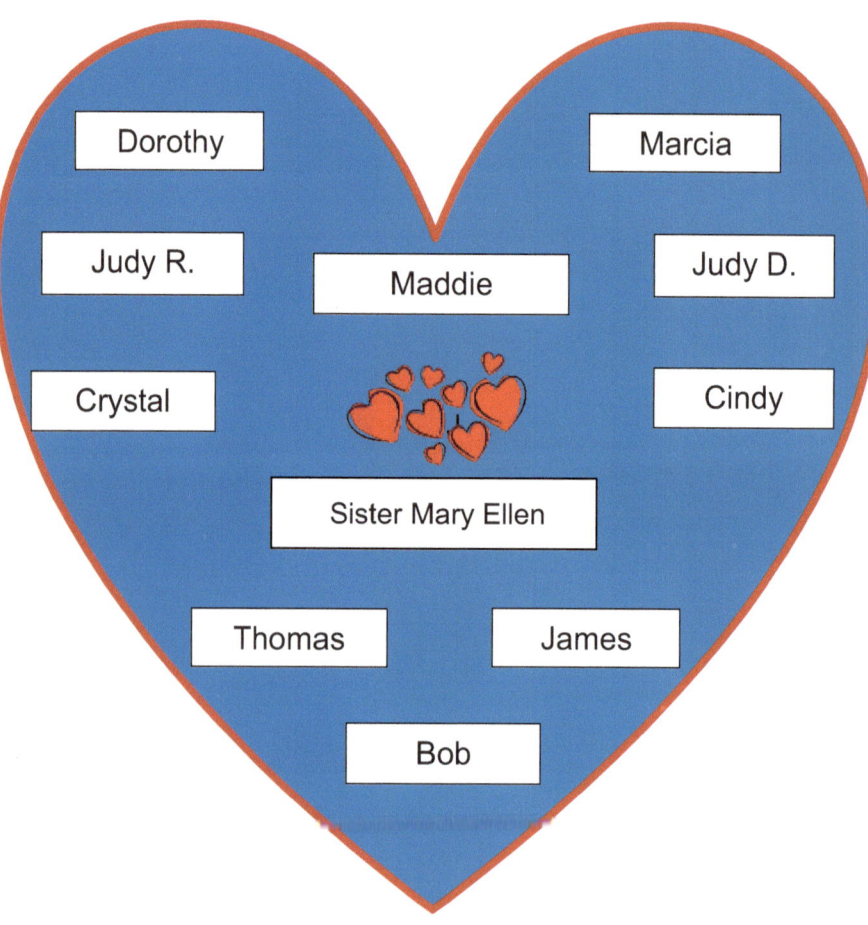

ntroduction

Introduction by Nancy S. Calumet

There is something irresistibly exciting about receiving a love letter from my husband who is in Heaven.

We are sharing our letters with so many readers to demonstrate that "life goes on" after physical death, and true love grows, deepens, and expands.

In the beginning, we started with an attraction that went beyond the physical aspects. We shared a deeply held respect and admiration for one another.

Adjectives which describe him are magnanimous, bright, charismatic, down to earth, and good looking.

We met in the mid nineteen-sixties. I was working as a young nurse at Columbus Hospital in Chicago. Tom was working as a commodity broker at the Board of Trade.

One morning, Tom was admitted to my nursing unit having sustained a mild heart attack.

The treatment in those days was a month of bedrest.

His physician ordered a private room and no phone calls or visitors. This prescription provided a much-needed rest and a stress-free environment in which to heal.

As head nurse, I remember assigning my best nurses to care for him. Tom was grateful for any little thing we did for him.

After that experience, he took much better care of his health, and we went on to share an exclusive relationship. We were married on Little Christmas in Evanston, Illinois by our friend, the judge, Dave Shields. Our friends and family were with us. Wedding vows once spoken to me meant "forever," but now I see "till death do us part" is a misnomer since we are still together.

Tom and I were not profoundly religious, rather, we are deeply spiritual. His death in 1990 was shocking to me, to his family, and to our friends. He died without warning, peacefully in his sleep.

If you have lost a loved one, you know we walk around in a state of shock and disbelief as in a fog bank. The brightest star in our quilt is gone. Life as we know it is turned upside down. Despite our having family and friends, depression, fear, and loneliness set in. Here is where KOKO comes in—we keep on keeping on. Faith and our conception of a hereafter bring us solace.

I wrote a poem about it, *Solo Flight,* which was published years later in my collection, *Gems,* as follows:

Solo Flight

His soul left sometime in the
*   early hours of winter's night*

His body found warm to
*   loving touch tucked silent*
*   beneath an afghan tomb*

Respirations ended
* silence surrounds as first*
*   the cat and then his wife*
*   reach his side to close*
*   his eyes and kiss his lips*

Softly whispered prayers
*   rise up to meet the*
*   incandescent blue white light*
*   hanging over his frame as*
*   angels vie to take him home*

Following Tom's funeral, I went right back to work. I was an assistant director of a medical quality assurance unit for the State of Illinois.

Nine months later, I moved from Chicago to Springfield, Illinois, near Taylorville, Illinois, where I grew up. My mother relocated and shared my new home for the next eighteen years. During this time, I made new friends, renewed old acquaintances, started writing poetry, and embraced Reiki as a way to self-heal. Tom was always in my heart and I felt he was nearby.

For the past thirty years, I have been on a quest to discover everything I could learn about the spirit world. I read extensively and met many highly evolved souls along the way. About five years ago I met Marcia McMahon and James Murray. Through James, I got to know his father, Robert Murray, who is now in Heaven with Tom.

Robert is the author of *The Stars Still Shine: An Afterlife Journey,* a book about the afterlife journey of his son-in-law, Michael, who was hit and killed on his way home one night. Michael immediately reached out to Robert, a gifted psychic, who wrote down Michael's words verbatim, giving us a glimpse of the day-by-day experiences Michael was having.

Why did God bring these people into my life? I think it was to reunite Tom and me, and, maybe, so this book would be written. It was also a gift to two lonely souls who do much better together than apart.

Tom and I invite you along on our journey. Feel the love, touch the possibilities, and enjoy the trip!

Love, Nancy

ntroduction

Introduction by Thomas Anthony Calumet

Hello,

This is Nancy's husband, Tom, coming to you from Heaven, where I have been living for the past thirty years. Since my transition, Nancy and I have always been in contact through our dreams though dreams are often hard to remember. Now a new dimension has been added to our love story—letter writing.

Nancy and I both realize we have been given a rare gift, and we credit God, and His angels on Earth, as well as in Heaven, for this miracle of written communication.

An actual letter can be held in one's hands, read and reread, savored, and cherished. Our letters allow us to stay current, anticipate one another's needs, and to offer support, advice, and loving guidance.

While our life together on Earth was amazing, these past five years have felt like we are still on a second honeymoon.

When I first arrived here, there was a period of adjustment to this new "life". I felt like I should get a job, but I learned that no one was hiring. I spent many years not working, just drifting. And then my life virtually exploded in a variety of new ways when Nancy became an active participant in my life here

I had been living in an apartment since I arrived and did not like it much. Then our friend, Bob Murray, invited me to see this house I am living in now. He sent a friend of his over to make the arrangements. I asked the price, and the man said it does not work that way here.

You don't have to pay to acquire a house. They are available for free, but you have to take care of it and maintain it. I accepted his explanation and "bought" this house without payment.

I never dreamed I would be living in a house again and loving it! My house is a small, Arts and Crafts style cottage. It has a small kitchen, dining room, living room with a stone fireplace, two bedrooms, and a full bath. I have no close neighbors, but I live on a paved street.

I am surrounded by green grass. In the front yard, there are several flower beds with begonias, daffodils, tulips, and other flowering varieties. I have a rural mailbox which stands at the opening of a picket fence. All my letters from Nancy arrive in this mailbox. I have a little red flag that is raised when I get mail. This is always exciting, and I never take it for granted. I just accept this wondrous gift that keeps on giving.

Oh, the back yard is large and surrounded by a wooden fence. I have a vegetable garden and grow carrots, tomatoes, potatoes, turnips, cauliflower, asparagus, zucchini, and string beans.

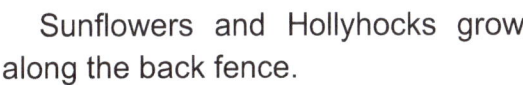

Sunflowers and Hollyhocks grow along the back fence.

We have a hot tub and a merry-go-round in this area which we enjoy when Nancy visits.

There is a rustic shed where we keep our bikes. We enjoy many activities together including walks in the park, live entertainment, theater in town, cookouts, and some entertaining.

To get here, Nancy soul-travels. Her physical body is asleep at home. We share intimate moments which are as desirable and pleasurable as on Earth. To say any more would be too personal.

I now have a job that I love, and you will hear more about it as you read our letters.

One spirit deserves special mention. Murial is my housekeeper and has been a "guiding light" in my life here. She sees to the correspondence and the packages Nancy sends. There are framed pictures of Nancy and me, and of relatives, hanging in the house. They, along with personal treasures and keepsakes, placed around the house, give it a warm, cozy feeling. Murial serves my breakfast and dinner hot every day at home. Nancy develops the menus.

Our dear friend and my scribe who writes up my letters and sends them to Nancy is James Murray. James is the connecting link in our story, and we could not do this without him.

I am still Nancy's husband, and she is my darling wife. Time and distance have not changed that. If anything, we are closer and more in love than ever.

So please sit back and enjoy the read. As your companions, we are with you along the way.

Allow our book to take you in a direction which is most important to you in your life.

Yours truly,
Tom

urial

Original watercolor by Marcia McMahon
www.marymagalenesmesage.com

Love letters between Tom in Heaven and Nancy on Earth

By Nancy S. Calumet

oreword

Between Heaven and Earth, Tom and Nancy are connected by love. A few years ago, James Murray began transcribing Tom's words for Nancy. The love-letter exchange continues to this very day. James is able to communicate with Tom and others who have crossed over. He hears their voices and describes what he sees in their surroundings. At his computer, he types their messages. He also draws what he "sees" during his visits. James is a professionally trained graphic artist who has been drawing most of his life. As a young child, even before he could speak, he was creating "little" pictures to communicate. To learn more about James and his contributions to his father, Robert Murray's, published works, visit:

http://www.TheStarsStillShine.com

James Murray, channel, and psychic artist

September 30, 2017

Nancy Wrote

Our letters began with the release of my book, *Gems: A Collection of Dream-time Poetry*, in which I penned about extraordinary "out-of-body," or "soul-travel" experiences of visiting in Heaven. I was astounded to learn that my book was actually showing up in Heaven.

On September 30, 2017
James Murray Wrote:

Dear Nancy,

After all the hard work, congratulations on the publication of your new book. I found it on Amazon.com.

My father [Robert Murray[1]] says, "Hello Nancy."

Tom [Calumet] immediately wanted to have a copy. He said, "I know the author." He also said he is a proud husband and just raised his glass to you! Word is getting around Heaven as well. Congratulations! [Signed,] Bob

Signed
James

---

[1] Robert Murray, 1935—2015, author of *The Stars Still Shine: An Afterlife Journey*, and subsequent books, was a psychic and afterlife communicator.

HEAVEN-SENT LOVE LETTERS by Nancy S. Calumet

March 20, 2018

My dear Nancy,

It is great to be able to communicate with you, thanks to our dear friends, James, and Bob who is here for me on this side.

I have been quite busy lately working as a volunteer at a homeless shelter. It may shock you to hear we have homeless people here, but people cross over as they are. They tell me I am doing a great job. Some are cranky, but I get along with them quite well. In fact, they call me Buddy. Some say they don't deserve a roof over their heads, but I say," Yes you do!" I don't try to convince them they are dead; that will come with time. They have mental and emotional hang-ups, but we have psychologists, psychiatrists, and social workers to treat them.

On to my next topic: I have planted some flowers, outside my little house, which bring much color. There is no shoveling snow here, no lawn to mow, and no need to water, to name a few perks.

If it were possible, I would send you a big bouquet for Easter.

I visited your folks recently. They are both fine.

That's all I have for now. I very much look forward to your next letter.

Oh, James reminded me you asked, 'Where is Heaven?' I can't say where it is, but it seems like I took a vacation and ended up on a remote island. Bob says "It is not far away.

We share the same space, even though we don't see one another in the physical form."

I see James is getting weary from writing my letter, so I will close for now.

Lots of love, kisses, and hugs,
Yours,
Tom

October 20, 2017

Nancy made a list of forty-six people in Heaven she wanted her book to go to and mailed the list to James. To her amazement, her handwritten letter appeared on Tom's bedside table.

So, how did it get there?

Our Angel Messenger

I knew I was getting help from Heaven when I learned my letters were going directly to Tom's mailbox.

Tom said, "Each letter looks like a page from a book and has little embellishments in the margins."

I thought *if I can send letters maybe I can send pictures,* and so I gathered some favorites and mentally sent them.

He informed me the pictures arrived in a large envelope with stickers saying, "Do not bend." Inside there was cardboard to protect the pictures! He was thrilled, of course, and had them framed.

We now knew we had our own angel and decided to name her Murial.

In order to mention her in this book, I asked Tom to get her permission first. The next day there was a note on his desk:

Dear Thomas and Nancy,

I believe this is the first time I have written to you.

You have asked for my permission to use my name in your book.

You have my consent in any form you see fit for your writings.

I trust your judgment.

Love and affection,

Murial

HEAVEN-SENT LOVE LETTERS by Nancy S. Calumet

She wrote the note on parchment paper with a quill and ink.

"Her penmanship is dazzling," Tom said. He has never seen anything like it before.

Although he has not seen her, Tom knows she is there. His refrigerator is always stocked along with his pantry. His house stays cleaned. Breakfast and dinner are served hot.

Murial is our jewel and we thank God for lending her to us.

She is noted as The Angel of Flowers, Peace, Gardens, Open Heart, and Healing.

We love and thank you, dear Murial.
Thomas and Nancy

October 20, 2017
Tom Wrote:

Hi Nancy,

I have your list. It appeared on my nightstand. So, I am your book distributor up here.

I took a copy to those I know, but I asked Bob what to do about the rest.

He suggested I take the list and books to the library. They will call the people in, and they will know the book is a gift from you.

Love,
Tom

March 24, 2018
Nancy's Letter

My dearest Tom,

Let us thank God for James and the miracle of our communications!

I will be staying here so long as I have something to contribute.

How are you today, my darling?

Serving the homeless is not only noble, but also something I know you are very good at.

You always had a compassionate heart and the ability to relate to all kinds of people.

The priest at your funeral mass said your legacy to your friends was "Keep it Simple." He also said you have the unique ability to pare down complex subject matters making it understandable to the rest of us.

I will close for now.

All my love,
Nancy

April 11, 2018
A Letter from Tom

My dear Nancy,

I am sending my love to you from here. As James may have told you, I am continuing to keep busy at the shelter.

It's a great place to work, and I enjoy being with the people. I don't really like to call them homeless. I consider them all friends which puts me at a level where I can connect with them. I don't really consider it a job.

There was a birthday party for a new friend in the shelter. He, Carlos, arrived a short time ago.

Yes, birthdays are still celebrated here. He sat in silence during the entire time. By the end of the day, he told me he was happy someone cared. He wished he were not in this situation, but he will adjust and move on in his new "life."

No one knows when that will be, but they say to give him time.

My flowers are doing very well. I don't know how the growing and blooming works. It just does.

I hope you received my bouquet. If not, I will try again. I will write again. It has been wonderful communicating with you.

Much love,
Tom
xxx oo xxx oo

April 11, 2018
Nancy Wrote to James

Dear James,

I notice Tom does not answer all my questions. Are they too mundane for someone as advanced as he is? It seems to take a month for our letters to come full circle, so I am starting now on a letter for his May birthday.

Best,
Nancy

Tom Stepped in to Explain

Nancy, I am sorry I am missing some of your questions. They are not mundane at all! I will begin to keep them in front of me, and James will also keep a list, so between us we don't miss anything.

Lots of love,
Tom
XXX OO XXX OO

April 14, 2018
Nancy Wrote

Gee, you are both so sensitive to my feelings! Thank you.

Tom, it's just that I was beginning to think you may have changed beyond my recognition.

How about an assignment?

Send me three songs expressing our love. I will start:

> *Unforgettable*
> *I Wish You Love*
> *Tangerine*

Love always,
Nancy

HEAVEN-SENT LOVE LETTERS by Nancy S. Calumet

May 14, 2018

Nancy Wrote a Poem and Birthday Letter to Tom

My darling Tom,

I wrote a new poem to celebrate your birthday.

But first how old are you now? Have you continued to age, or have you reversed the process?

I read in "James's newsletter that Frank Sinatra is with Ava, and they are both "re-youthing."

Do you remember that you planned to take me to Paris in April 1990? I still want to take that trip with you someday.

Is Bugsy with you? I had a vision of you holding him in your arms. He was such a beautiful Maine Coon cat!

And now here is your poem:

Universe of One

Stars falling from the sky

Our eyes lock in wonder

Hearts beating as one the only sound

From a place of unconditional love

an unbreakable bond bridges our two worlds

into one vast sea of remembrance.

On your birthday I celebrate the best in you

And wish you love

May 20, 2018
Tom Wrote

My dear Nancy,

Here are my three songs:

> *Can't Stop Falling in Love with You*, by Elvis
> *I'll Be Seeing You*, by Billie Holiday
> *What A Wonderful World*, by Louis Armstrong

I am influenced by entertainers I see perform at "The Club", a nightclub over here where they still sing for an audience.

Thank you, my dear, for the poem. It rings true as to what we had on Earth and still have. I am so happy to receive your poem and letter. It warms my heart.

You asked, "How old am I?"

I am in my thirties as I liked that age best when I was alive. I like the maturity of my thirties as I am not too young, but old enough to say I have some life experience.

(Nancy inserted:)

[I am told our soul body looks like our physical body unless we chose to change our appearance. Tom said he can't tell any difference. Looks like his body to him. When I travel to visit him, I always pick my early thirties to travel in. No point taking my seventy-eight-year-old body if I don't have to. By the way, they shower, shave, use the bathroom etc. just like they did here. Good to know, eh?]

(Tom continued:)

I remember our planned trip to Paris like it was yesterday. We can still make that trip while you're asleep and your soul flies free. Let's work on that.

I was keeping an eye on you while you were sick. It's no fun being ill, and I am glad you're recovered.

Please keep up your health for me.

It's strange that you mentioned Bugsy. Yes, he is here with me. He likes to sit on my lap and loves it when you visit.

Folks here heard I'm having a birthday, and they are planning my party, streamers, and all.

I had better go now. I'm looking forward to your letters and more.

Sending all my love to you,
Your Tom

xxx oo xxx oo

May 27, 2018
Nancy's Letter to Tom

Hello Thomas, my love,

When I last visited, you recognized the scent I was wearing, No5 CHANEL Paris, the same one you bought me when on Earth.

In a recent reading with Marcia, you came through and sent a dozen red roses, your love, and your support. Thank you, darling.

You know I would do anything you ask me to do, so yes, I will take better care of my health.

It is through my dreams, I am aware of our visits. I want to share my journal notes with you from my dream-time experience of December 2002.

Nancy's note: I bought a lovely new sofa, just before Christmas, and lay down just to test it out. I was instantly asleep.

I flew out through my living room window, and there in my courtyard sat a little white house. There was a little table with two chairs on the front patio, and you were there.

It gave me such a wonderful feeling of peace, safety, and protection to know you were nearby. Do you recall this?

More later.

Love,
Nancy

June 26, 2018
A Letter from Tom

Dear Nancy, my love,

I am always excited to connect with you. The letter and note exchanges are amazing. It's not quite the same as saying this in person, but it is a wonderful thing that we have, and I am grateful to you and to James.

I do remember your visit that day. It was early evening, and I gave you a little tour of my house.

I am happy you keep journal notes otherwise that visit would be forgotten.

I have been asked to help out at the hospital to make newcomers feel more comfortable in their new surroundings. So when I am free, I am part of the Welcoming Committee.

I found two more of your cats, who have crossed over, hanging around outside. I invited them in, and they seem right at home. Yes, I can say they moved in. I think they sense your energy and know I need the company.

I have added your song, *I'm Your Man,* to our collection, by Leonard Cohen. You probably know that he arrived here not long ago. Great choice. I am in the process of gathering three more songs. I want them to be special.

I will close for now and send you all my love, Nancy.

Much love from Tom

xxx oo xxx oo

June 26, 2018
Nancy Sent a Note to Tom

Darling Tom,

Interesting that we both chose the song *Unforgettable.* When I first moved to Springfield, I joined a widow's support group at the West Side Christian Church. On my way home from a meeting, that song came on the radio, and the floodgates opened. I began sobbing causing me to have to pull over to the side of the road.

You see, I had buried the pain of losing you so deeply that I was unable to cry until I heard that song! Crying is cleansing, but I had suppressed it. This was a big breakthrough for me.

At this moment, I miss you so much, it feels like I have a hole in my heart, and it burns like a heartburn.

No doubt it would be worse if I could not share this with you.

On a lighter note I love your song choice, *Dancing Cheek to Cheek.* It reminds me of you dancing me across the floor at the Palmer House. We were the last couple on the dance floor, and the band played on just for us. So sweet!

I will leave you with this beautiful thought as written in the words of Leonard Cohen. He expressed exactly how I feel.

"I love you a thousand kisses deep."

Nancy
P.S.
The small orange and white cat is named Little Al, and the big fluffy orange one is Baby.

July 25, 2018
Tom Wrote

My dearest Nancy,

It has been a while, but you know James has been busy. I am very happy he is available now to take down my words to you.

I hear your voice off and on. Guess I forgot to mention this before. This is happening during the day when I am awake. It is not easy to describe what I hear, but it is something like hearing someone talking from another room in your home. I really love hearing your voice!

Other people I may be with at the time do not hear you. Only I hear you. And I only pick up parts of a conversation.

I went to visit your folks a few weeks ago. They are fine and send their love to you.

Waltz tunes are becoming a favorite of mine. I know we both love music. I heard Bing Crosby sing at The Club recently. One memorable song was *Where the Blue of the Night*. Let's add this one to our list.

I had an interesting encounter with Leonard Cohen. We literally ran into one another as I was going in, and he was leaving The Club.

He said, "Sorry my friend, I did not see you."

Before we moved on, I said "No problem, I'm okay." I recognized him from his flyers posted around town.

I have to go now, but I am always thinking of you.

Love, love, love from your Thomas

xxx oo xxx oo

HEAVEN-SENT LOVE LETTERS by Nancy S. Calumet

July 26, 2018
Nancy Wrote

Darling Tom,

First, thank you and James for your letter.

It's very interesting that you can hear my voice.

If you could read my mind, you would know I say, "I love you," a dozen times a day.

I got my first dog after I moved to Springfield. She was a chocolate lab puppy, and I named her Coco Chanel Calumet. I failed to have her trained properly, so we called her the wild child. I gave her to my brother, Jim, and he took her with him to South Dakota when he got a teaching position at Sinte Gleska University in Mission, SD. Coco crossed over many years ago, and I mention this to ask you to track down her whereabouts.

Tom Stepped in to Reply

I was invited to your folks' home for dinner, and I met your Aunt Mary Frances and her companion who are raising Coco. I took her outside for a walk to do her duty. Things operate here very much like they do on Earth. This is just one example.

Rest assured she is in loving hands, looks good, and appears well trained and happy.

Nancy Closed

I will close now with the knowledge she is in good hands.

All my love,
Nancy

August 30, 2018
A Letter from Tom

My dearest Nancy,

Sorry for the delay with this letter; I was ready, but James has been very busy of late. It gives me great pleasure to write to you.

You mentioned aches and pains and asked if we experience them here. The answer is: yes, I do have an occasional headache and minor muscle pain. I have a pain reliever in my medicine cabinet to take at times like that.

Someone said I can live here entirely pain free, but it gives me and everyone else here something to complain about. We compare notes, and it makes us feel like we are still human and still on planet Earth! It also makes your day when you do feel like a million.

You mentioned both your knees are bone on bone. Do whatever you have to do to take care of that. I am no doctor, but don't forego anything. If it means knee replacements, then that is what you will need to do. You will get through it, and I am here for you whatever you decide. If you can prevent an operation, even better. I will keep you walking!

Your new hair cut is amazing, but more than amazing. Stunning is a better word for all of you. Do you remember us celebrating your birthday over here? I presented you with a dozen red roses and some confections. It was a VERY important date. I even bought a new suit for the occasion. I took you to a show, and we did some dancing to the strings of Glenn Miller and His Orchestra. *When You're Smiling* was one of the tunes we danced to. We both had a great time, short but wonderful!

And now an interesting tidbit from the shelter: A man arrived here, and he looked just like Jesus. He was wearing a long robe and had a beard. He immediately said, "I am not Him." He had a Portuguese accent. He wondered if he was in Portuguese Heaven. One sure meets interesting people here.

I will end my letter by sending you a whole basket of flowers and all my love on this beautiful Sunday.

Have a wonderful day, my dear.

Lots of love, hugs, and kisses,
Your Tom

HEAVEN-SENT LOVE LETTERS by Nancy S. Calumet

September 5, 2018.
Nancy Wrote

My darling husband, Tom,

It was with great joy and gratitude that I received your letter Sunday.

Sounds like my birthday spent with you was the best ever, and I thank you for a wonderful night out on the town, and Glenn Miller to boot—WOW! Thanks for the replay. As you know, I rarely remember our times together.

I have an appointment tomorrow with an orthopedic doctor, and we will be doing injections first to see if that helps.

What an interesting story about the Jesus look-alike! I look forward to meeting the real Jesus someday. Perhaps we will invite him, Saint Luke, and Saint Jude over for breakfast. They are all members of my healing team whom I call for when I get a prayer/healing request.

I recall reading in Bob's book that Michael was having a party when Jesus and a few of His companions strolled in and mingled for a while. That's where I got this idea. What do you think?

All my love to you,
Nancy

September 13 2018

Nancy Wrote a Note to James

Dear James,

I understand the process you use to transcribe Tom's letters to me, but what do you have to do with my letters back to him?

Wishing you a good day,
Best,
Nancy

James's Father, Bob Murray, Responded

Nancy, you do all the work. When you focus on a letter or a note, it somehow finds its way to Tom.

He is receiving them. Tom has a few words for you now.

Tom Wrote:

Nancy,
Remember the mailbox in front of my house? The little red flag is raised often, and your notes and letters are placed carefully inside. You are a master at writing them. It's always a huge thrill to receive one of your letters. How they arrive is a miracle. I think love has wings, and your love carries your words to me on paper.

Bob agrees and explained: we have an energy that transcends our worlds and does amazing things. I think you know what I am saying.

Lots of love, hugs, and kisses back to you, Nancy,
Your Tom

September 15, 2018
A Note from Nancy

Darling Tom,

I feel like I visited last night. I woke up suddenly at 4:00 a.m. and checked the time.

Watch your mail. I sent three photos yesterday.

Fall is here, and today is a crisp, clear, fall day. Are you able to enjoy the seasons there?

For all I know, I may be here for many, many, more years. What do you think about this?

I will leave you with this thought:

The power of Christ gives me strength,
The Holy Spirit brings me joy.

Sending all my love,
Nancy

September 18, 2018
A Note from Nancy

Dearest Tom,

I hope to hear from you soon.

I love the musical, *Jersey Boys,* about Frankie Valli and the Four Seasons. Let's add this song to our list:

Can't Take My Eyes Off of You.

How we missed seeing them in the sixties, I will never know!

It makes me very happy knowing you are in such a good place.

When I replay a scene from our life together, I can feel all of the emotions over again.

Closing for now,
Much love,
Nancy

September 20. 2018
A Note from Tom

My dear Nancy,

I receive every note and letter you send. My mailbox is full of love.

Each and every day I am sending all my love, hugs, and kisses, back to you.

Have a wonderful day, and you will be receiving a letter from me soon.

Yours,
Tom

October 2, 2018
A Note from Nancy

Good morning, dear Tom,

Polly, the cat, and I went on a little adventure early this a.m.

It was about daybreak when she wanted to go outside, and I decided to go with her.

We walked around and explored some of her favorite spots. I hugged a tree, and she rolled around in the dirt. We both had great fun!

All my love,
Nancy

HEAVEN-SENT LOVE LETTERS by Nancy S. Calumet

Tom's October Letter to Nancy

My dear, Nancy,

I cherish every note and letter from you.

I met your Grandpa Elzior at a gathering at your folks' home. He walked up and introduced himself to me. Very interesting fellow. We had quite a long conversation. I can see where your great love for the U.P.[2] comes from.

Nancy, I don't think one of your letters has been lost. Love makes sure they arrive safely along with your determination and the help of the angels. You are the master more than the postmaster.

You talked about your transition. Don't hurry home on my account. I mean, as much as I would love to have you with me, you have a full schedule ahead of you in the coming years—things you must do there. I want to allow you to do just that.

When your time is up, I will be the first to greet you at the gate. Actually, I have not seen any pearly gates here, but I will be there to welcome you no matter where it is. In the meantime, go with the flow, my dear.

I recall much from our visits, and you seem to be remembering more, too. When we meet, it is very special. We seem to just pick up where we left off. When I lie down at night, I cannot always control all I do. If we miss one another some nights, there will always be other opportunities when the time is right and the stars all line up, etc. Know this much: What we have is amazing!

I have the pictures you sent. Thank you! It's funny that they arrived in a large envelope with lots of written stickers. I opened it, and there you were in two of the pictures. I have to be honest, I shed some tears. I held them close to my heart and wept. It was a wonderful gift. The next day, I went to town to find a frame

---

[2] Michigan's Upper Peninsula

HEAVEN-SENT LOVE LETTERS by Nancy S. Calumet

shop. I stopped a man and asked if he knew where I could find one. He directed me down the street and one block over to the place of a friend, who is an artist.

As I approached the place, there was an older woman sitting in a chair. She spoke first and asked, "How may I help you, young man?"

I told her I had some cherished photos I wanted to frame. She invited me inside and pointed to a corner where I chose from a great variety. I asked her what I owed.

She said, "It's a gift. You pay it forward as I don't accept payment."

By the way, the pictures look beautiful hanging in the house in their new frames.

I have not seen any leaves falling or turning color. I will have to look into that. You asked if I had days off from the shelter. Yes, once in a while, but if they ask me to come in, I always oblige.

What we have with our letters and visits between our two worlds is wonderful and amazing. James is doing a great job of keeping my letters flowing.

You mentioned you have been going to bed earlier and sleeping longer. That is due to your Cortisone injections. I am glad they are working so far. I probably don't get enough sleep. I am never tired during the day, but by nighttime, I am tired. I think that's natural. My body tells me when my energy level is low. So, we get tired here, even though we no longer have our physical bodies—although I still feel like I have one. In actuality, I am now living in my soul-body.

I will send my next installment soon. In the meantime, I am sending you a whole world of love, today and every day. We are always together no matter the time of day or location.

Yours,
Tom

October 8, 2018
Nancy Wrote

Dearest Thomas,

I believe we have an angel messenger. I say this because of the way you described the envelope, stickers, and packing material with the photographs. That was not in my thinking.

I have read of an ancient gift, long forgotten, where unseen spirit hands send cards and letters embellished with little drawings in the margins. Perhaps this is what is happening for us with our angel-helper Murial.

I was pleased you met my Grandpa Elzior. I lived with him and my Grandma Irene during the Second World War when my dad was in the service, and my mom worked as a nurse in a nearby town in the Upper Peninsula of Michigan.

That was during my most formative years, ages one through four. I was in the best of hands.

I first heard the phrase, "Pay it forward," here recently, and find it interesting and a delightful way to keep "good" flowing. I believe that in Heaven all things are possible and wishes are granted. So it seems possible we can have fall leaves, falling snowflakes, and soft feminine rain, if only for a short time.

I describe soul-travel as flying because that's what it feels like to me. One morning, I felt myself zooming over the Congress Expressway in Chicago on my way home. I saw the traffic backed up with cars bumper-to-bumper with people on their way to work, and the next thing I woke up to my alarm clock set to get me up for work. That gave me a vivid window into how soul-travel works. That all took place in an instant.

I think you know how much your letters mean to me.

Till we meet in our dreams, I send my love, hugs, and kisses,

Nancy

October 12, 2018
Nancy Wrote a Note

Darling Tom,

It feels like we visited last night. I woke up as we were kissing goodbye.

Tom, I wonder if you ever get bored.

When I feel bored, I get busy and often begin reading a book.

A little book I often turn to is called *The Impersonal Life,* by Joseph S. Benner, written in 1914 and still being published by DeVorss Publications. This work records words given through Joseph from God.

I will share a passage from page 198 that I read today,

> "You, who have risen above Desire, you who no longer seek a Master or a Teacher, …but are abiding in the faith of My Eternal Presence … for you I have in store a meeting and a communion, which will bring to your Soul such joy and blessing as your human mind is incapable of conceiving."

Perhaps this passage reflects the gift we have received. What do you think?

I love you so much,
Nancy

October 20, 2018
Nancy Wrote

Dearest Tom,

By Earth standards you have been gone a long time, but to me it seems like yesterday when you were here with me.

I recall our tickets to Cancun arrived on the day you died. Our friends, Jim and Mary Lou, insisted I go with them as planned, and I agreed.

On the plane Jimmy said, "Nancy, you sit with Mary Lou, and I will sit behind you with my buddy, Tom."

He gave you the window seat and we felt like you were with us.

Enough of the trip down memory lane.

My love for you grows stronger every day. I could fill a room with it. You are surrounded by my love every place you go. You walk through it, breathe it in, and feel it in every word I send you.

Nancy

November 1, 2018
A Note from Tom

James Wrote:
Nancy, Tom has a few words for you today.

Tom Continued:
Nancy, my love,

James and I are in the midst of writing a letter to a beautiful lady.

Hang in there. It's a work in progress.

Sending you all my love,

Yours,

Tom

Tom's November Letter

Nancy, my love,

It's been a while, and now I have a chance to send you my words.

The pictures you sent appear to have been enlarged to size nine by twelve and are now framed and hanging in my house.

You asked if I ever get bored. The answer is, I don't have time. My life here does not know that word.

Although, when I first arrived here that may have been a factor, I soon learned from others that one must keep busy.

That said, I always have time for you! Our time together is VERY precious.

Don't get me started on pizza! (I'm smiling.) I walk to the local Pizzeria in town a few times a week. No weight gain here or cholesterol to worry about.

Sometimes I try cooking at home. Someone is making grocery deliveries when I am not here. This may sound strange, but this is Heaven, after all.

On my way home from work, I made a stop to check in with your folks. I believe you sent them a picture, and they have it hanging. They were quite surprised and feel it came from God. They think you must have an office in His house.

James and I were looking over the passage you sent, and YES, we are living that special life! It is hard to describe what we're experiencing. No one else seems to be doing it. Although, I hesitate to ask around as they might look at me funny. Sometimes I, too, think you're working out of God's office.

HEAVEN-SENT LOVE LETTERS by Nancy S. Calumet

I want to thank you, my dear, for sending me that special passage. Don't hold back when you want to say something.

I try to send subliminal thoughts and pictures to you. As you do your meditation, see if you can receive them.

Please don't get frustrated, my dear. Bob tells me to be patient and let things come when they come. He said time is different here, and like a message in a bottle, the thought might be received sometime later.

He added we always have his son, James, and him to help us with our connection.

On another subject, I am so happy you made the trip with Jimmy and Mary Lou. I was there in spirit during that trip.

I had a ticket, and I was determined to be around despite the circumstances.

I am thrilled with our connection now. I have so much more to say, but I will be back soon.

For now, I love you more than anything. We share a very special love. Keep smiling.

Sending a world of hugs and kisses.

Yours,

Tom

November 17, 2018
Nancy Wrote,

Good morning, my dear husband, Tom.

With your departure, I think I told you, I began to explore all things spiritual and metaphysical.

I joined an "In Search of God" group. We read from a book containing Edgar Casey's teachings.

That study led me to the Spiritualist Church in LeRoy, Illinois, where part of the service was devoted to receiving a message from Spirit. One Sunday, the minister asked if he could come to me. He said, "You have a book on your shelf you are supposed to read, and he held up a six by eight, black book.

I looked upstairs and downstairs on my bookshelves and found no book of that description. Then I called him.

He asked, "Have you looked in the basement?" That is where I found it.

When I read that book, these words popped out at me, "Every morning one is to ask, 'Lord, what would thou have me do today?' Say this three times and mean it!"

As I began saying these words, I did not notice much difference in my life. However I did not give up saying them.

Then, about five years ago, I began to listen to what I was saying, and then some wonderful wisdom and inspiration began to flow into me. I felt connected to my source! It was like the links of a beautiful gold chain connected what, before, were coincidences into a solid configuration, and I became a real, living person God could count on to do His will.

Years of searching, and not finding, began to coalesce into one vast sea

of color. This, Tom, has made me happier than ever, leading me back to you.

I wish you a Happy Thanksgiving, my dear, and hope to make a visit.

I wonder if you have heard of Dr. Wayne Dwyer, who has now crossed over. I just listened to one of his lectures on PBS. He does a great I AM meditation. I think you would like him.

Sending all my love,
Nancy

November 24, 2018
A Note from Nancy

Dearest Thomas,

I'm sending you all my love, a big hug and kiss this a.m.

I had this incredible dream of this grand party for me when I cross over.

You were standing in this large atrium waiting for my arrival. The floor was black and white tile. Above you there was a three-tiered dining room overlooking the lobby. There was a little candle lamp on each table. There were tables for two, four, six, and eight, and all were packed with guests. I was sitting at a table-for-two and watching.

Suddenly, the massive oak door flew open, and I strode in like a lioness, tanned, blond, wearing a white toga. You were in tails. I walked right into your waiting arms, and you twirled me around, and the crowd went wild! It took me by surprise, as it dawned on me that it was ME! Oh, what a party we have to look forward to! I did not really recognize any of the guests, but I think they were former patients I had taken care of, and friends, and family.

I sure miss you today more than usual. I am thinking about your laughter and dimpled cheeks.

I love you,
Nancy

HEAVEN-SENT LOVE LETTERS by Nancy S. Calumet

December 14, 2018
A Letter from Tom

My dear Nancy,

I wait anxiously and read every word you write. I keep your letters all in one binder.

After you recovered from your flu, you made a visit. You kept me busy bringing you hot beverages. You said, "Please, no cold drinks. I need to be warmed up." I got us a warm blanket from the closet, and we snuggled on the sofa.

There must have been something in our drinks because we fell asleep, and I don't remember much after that.

By the way, I know of Dr. Dwyer. He gives talks at our library here, but I have not yet attended. What does he talk about?

You mentioned your homecoming celebration here. You are like royalty here! A real celebrity to a growing list of souls, who have read your book and followed your healing work. You are the most incredible woman I know, and yes, I am fortunate to have you in my life! You have helped me and so many other people. I look forward to your arrival but don't pack your bags yet. I would like, more than anything to have you here, but as I have said before, you have so much more to do there.

You asked if I see my mom and dad. Yes, on occasion. They are stuck in bygone years. Nothing I can do about that.

Oh, I came home to a delightful surprise. A fully decorated Christmas tree was in my living room with wrapped gifts underneath it.

You and Murial have been busy! I will be awaiting your visit Christmas Eve.

I will end my letter by sending all my love to keep you warm on these cold winter nights. May all our days be bright.

Lots of love, hugs, and kisses,
Thomas
xxx oo xxx

January 2019
Tom Wrote

Nancy, my dear,

Our new year is off with a big bang.

Jesus accepted your invitation to breakfast at our home!

I received short notice that a visitor was coming because of your request.

I was at the Diaper Ranch[3] one morning a few days ago when one of the nursing sisters came over to me and said, "You have a visitor coming to see you shortly."

I asked, "Who, and where should I meet this person?"

She said, "Oh, you will recognize Him, but I will give you a hint. He loves children, but most importantly, He loves everyone and excludes no one. He will meet you right here. He will find you."

She left, and a short time later I felt a light tap on my shoulder. The tap was so gentle, and I felt an incredible amount of energy from His touch. I turned, and there was our friend, Jesus.

He said, "Hello, Thomas. Your friend Nancy sent an invitation for a breakfast at your home. We graciously accept her offer. I am including our friends and yours truly. When you are ready to host the breakfast, just call, and we will be there at the snap of your fingers. We are faster than light."

---

[3] Diaper Ranch: for young children, an afterlife residential hospital resembling a western American ranch and labeled the Diaper Ranch by Michael, or D.R. for short.

Jesus smiled, had a little laugh, and continued, "I see you have been a very busy man helping so many people. Continue your tireless work for humanity and thank you for taking the time today for my visit. I will see you soon and will let you continue with your work."

He shook my hand, gave me a hug, and waved goodbye. Although He did not mention His name, how could I not know who He is? I believe our friend, Michael, has met Him. I will have to ask him about it. I will get back to you soon with the date, plans, and actual visit.

All my love,
Your Tom

January 10, 2019
Tom Wrote

Our Visit and Breakfast with Jesus

Dearest Nancy,

Our breakfast with Jesus and His friends finally arrived, and you were there, or I should say, here!

I invited Michael, and Bob Murray. They helped put out the food. We had a few of the children come from the Diaper Ranch, and they sat together at a picnic table. We served buffet style in our backyard.

A great variety of dishes were laid out on long tables. We served Eggs Benedict, pancakes, French toast with fruit of all kinds, a large array of tea and coffee with coffee cakes, and muffins. Michael did bacon and sausage on the grill. He suggested having a round table with a white tablecloth for the adults which was set up under an apple tree in full bloom! The weather was perfect.

When all was ready, I made the call. I heard the front doorbell, and I went inside to answer the door. There stood Jesus, and He introduced Saints Luke, Jude, and Paul, although the saint word was not used.

I went down on my knees, and He said, "You are a very gracious host, Thomas," and indicated I should stand. Then we all exchanged handshakes and hugs of greeting. I escorted them all to the back yard and introduced them to everybody. Nancy, you were speechless! (You looked beautiful, by the way.)

You helped get the children started, and everyone served themselves. It was all good, and there was not a morsel of food left over. The conversation was lively with all chiming in about the food as we got acquainted.

Then Jesus said, "We thank you, Tom, Nancy, and Murial for this most delicious breakfast. We rarely receive personal invitations such as yours. We have had a wonderful time, and all the food was outstanding!"

Before they left to attend other activities, Jesus visited with the little children. He picked up a little girl, walked her over to us, and introduced her as Uma. He said, "She made this for us," and He placed an apple pie on the table. She told Jesus He has to come back and visit again. We all felt the love energy coming from that little girl.

Jesus and His friends were so gracious, relaxed, and seemingly delighted to be invited to our humble home. As we all said our goodbyes, we knew we had been especially blessed with their visit, and that we were not strangers, rather we were friends.

Interestingly, He thanked Murial. Though she was not seen, she had everything to do with preparing the meal.

So, I will close for now.

Nancy, I know you will have some questions, and I will answer all of them.

All my love, hugs, and kisses, my dear,
Your Tom

January 13, 2019
A Letter from Nancy

Dearest Thomas,

I am thrilled to receive your rendition of our visit with Jesus, Luke, Jude, and Paul.

You said I was speechless, and I guess I still am. The power of creative, inspired thought brought our idea into manifestation! Awesome!

I woke up to a winter wonderland with twelve inches of freshly fallen snow, still pristine and lovely to look upon. This is a day to order groceries online and have them delivered, a lovely service to be sure.

According to White Eagle, there is a temple in Heaven called "The Blue and White Temple of Healing" where soul-travelers go to receive a healing Rx from the angels of healing, as directed by Jesus. I sometimes ask to go there, just before falling asleep. I always wake up feeling relaxed and pain free. Have you heard of it or been there?

The color purple keeps coming up in your name and address once I hit my Send button. I wonder if it appears this way when you receive my letters in your mailbox.

I will close for today and send you all my love.

Nancy

January 20, 2019
A Letter from Tom

My dear Nancy,

Until you mentioned it, I was not familiar with any temples here. Bob did some research, and we went seeking the one you described. What we saw is not what others may see or experience. We were met at the door by a monk who asked what we were seeking and then he offered to give us a tour.

We saw people kneeling in prayer in large open rooms. The atmosphere was very holy, peaceful, and quiet.

Maybe I entered the wrong door, but I did not discover a blue and white room. However, the rooms seemed to expand and go on forever. Maybe one should ask for the White Eagle room. We were glad we went, and we were welcomed back anytime. Like so many things here, it's all a mystery to me!

On to another subject—that of past lives we have shared together—I have decided to investigate the Akashic records and see if I can add to the body of knowledge you have discovered.

At the library, I met a lady named Amanda who led me to a room and directed me to sit in a comfortable chair. She handed me a remote control. I was told to listen carefully to the instructions coming from speakers in the walls.

As I sat in the chair counting backward from one hundred, I was in a deep sleep halfway through.

I began my adventure walking through a town dating back to the turn of the century. I saw an American flag, so I knew I was in the USA. As I walked along the street, I came upon a general store with a sign "Galveston Town Hall".

HEAVEN-SENT LOVE LETTERS by Nancy S. Calumet

The streets were cobblestone, and I was in Texas. I looked down to see what I was wearing. Turned out to be a nice three-piece suit with a white shirt, bow tie, and black dress-shoes.

A well-dressed gentleman came up and introduced himself to me. He said, "We have been waiting for you, Mr. Leopold. Please follow me."

I followed him into a comfortable-looking room, where we met another man who said, "Our town is in tatters. We need you to help straighten out an urgent matter."

So now, I will summarize the rest. I am an elected, state-government official, and have been called in to help resolve an issue of high taxes. The citizens are up in arms about subsidizing their state government! I was very diplomatic and explained the need to keep the state operating. My name is Reginald Leopold. I will learn more in my next session.

You said I never asked you about Reiki, and then you went on to explain it quite well.

Could I learn to do it? Are there prerequisites? I am thinking it could be very useful to help some of the residents at the shelter who sometimes suffer from old injuries and past trauma. If you think I could use it to be of more help to them, I am all for it! Let me know what you think.

By the way, your letters come to me beautifully typed, but not from a typewriter. They look like they come out of a book, nicely decorated with hearts, flowers, angel motifs, etc., in vibrant colors ready for hanging.

Bugsy is quite the charmer. He greets me to welcome me home and likes to sit with me at the end of my day. Your other two cats are around, too, and I call them the "Felino Duo".

You and I have something very special, and I am so thankful to be able to rekindle our love and relationship.

I am sending you enough flowers to fill a room to brighten your day, along with all my love, hugs, and kisses.

Keep warm, my dear.

Your Thomas

Xxxoooxxxooo

January 22, 2019
A Letter from Nancy

My darling, Tom,

I enjoyed every word and sentiment in your last letter.

It pleases me you are interested in Reiki. Yes, this is something you can do.

Your desire and intention are the only prerequisites.

Next in importance is the selection of your Reiki Master Teacher. This person will be experienced, practical, and compatible with your energy. I am sure there will be many to choose from up there, and I am also available to teach a long-distance course. [For the record Tom picked me.]

Your course will be sent to you over a period of six weeks. All handouts, manuals, and assignments will arrive in your mailbox.

You will learn to give a self treatment, a full-body treatment to another person, and how to send a long-distance treatment to anyone in the Universe.

In your case, the sacred Attunement Ceremony transferring the Reiki Energy to you will be done on your surrogate—my Teddy Bear.

I will send your certificates to First and Second Degree to your mailbox.

[*Note....I will not be sharing any class material in this book. The Teachings are usually reserved for the classroom.

Teddy, by the way, has taken on the role of healing bear. Due to Tom's Attunement Ceremony, Teddy was filled with the Reiki Ray, and he glows transmitting the energy.

I took Teddy with me on a visit to see Tom, and he got left behind. Tom decided to take Teddy with him to the Diaper Ranch, and the kids fell in love with him. We asked Spirit to duplicate Teddy, so each child could have one of their own. Miniatures were created for the infants in their cribs. Needless to say, Teddy is now famous and resides in Heaven.

James has created an illustration of Teddy for our book. James traveled to the Diaper Ranch to see and to sketch Teddy. His brother-in-law, Michael, requested the enlarged sized Teddy so volunteers could sit in his lap and read to the children.]

And now a word about your last regression. I am sure with a name like Reginald, I called you Reggie at home. Sound familiar?

So, I will close for today.

Sending you all my love, hugs, and kisses,
Nancy

HEAVEN-SENT LOVE LETTERS by Nancy S. Calumet

February 14, 2019
A Valentine from Nancy

Darling Tom,

I am here with a poem to celebrate US! I wrote this poem for you some time ago. I was looking through pictures for our book when I found it among my notes. It is Untitled

> ℒove is not subtle
>
> rather like a thunderbolt
>
> ℒove is never outdone
>
> more like a rainbow after it rains
>
> ℒove creeps silently into the heart
>
> during the night
>
> In winter it keeps away the cold
>
> In autumn it mingles with the leaves
>
> In spring it bursts forth on butterfly wings
>
> In summer it sparkles in sunshine

So I wrote this poem thinking of you, my dear man!

Going through pictures took me down a lane of happy memories.

My brother, the poet, might say it needs an ending. I thought about it and decided to stop while I was ahead.

Awaiting my next love letter,
All my love,
Nancy

February 17, 2019
A Letter from Tom

My darling Nancy, my wife, my friend, my lover,

I framed the poem you sent, and it is hanging in the bedroom. It fits in nicely there in the frame! It reminds me of you ... us. It came on very nice paper stock and had some motifs added. Someone knew I was going to frame it! Murial?

You asked for a Reiki progress report. I saw the film you recommended about the chakras, at the library. I am feeling more confident in my abilities. I have two clients here at the shelter. One man is still suffering from arthritis in his back and hips. My hands get hot when I am treating him, so he started calling me "Hot Healing Hands". He said his pain subsided.

Another client suffers from migraines. She has also found relief. I give you all the credit along with my guides and angels for this gift you have given me. I have also been sending you treatments for your knees and lower back pain. Can you tell?

Feedback is always appreciated, especially from you, about all the people on Earth on whom we are combining our skills to treat. I have tried sending Reiki for two hours before I leave for work in the a.m. Sometimes, when you send me a new patient name, I might start a new person in the evening. I have never felt more vital and necessary as I do now, working with you, our guides, and our Reiki angels!

In closing, bo my Valentine! Sending all my love, hugs, and kisses.

Yours,

Thomas

February 28, 2019
A Letter from Tom

My dear Nancy,

My Reiki Certificates are now hanging in the hall outside my Reiki room.

I have been invited to use the Reiki Clinic here founded by your own true mentor and Reiki Master. This is a wonderful invitation, and one I will be glad to take advantage of. She said she has a job waiting for you when you cross over!

All my love to you, my Reiki Master Teacher. I still have a great deal to learn, but like you said, "Don't worry, it is your Reiki Guides and angels who are doing the work through you." I have already started by sending you an Rx.

How do you feel today?

I am having dinner at your folks' house this evening. I am not sure who else might be there. Your dad is a great cook and their gatherings are always enjoyable.

James has a lot on his agenda today, so I will close for now.

All my love,
Your Thomas

March 4, 2019
From Nancy to James

Dear James,

I have a question for your dad about Tiny Diamond, a Sheltie dog who was purchased from a shelter August 10, 1997, by my friend, Cindy.

Please forgive me if I am asking too much, but we were hoping for some feedback.

Bye for now, and I hope you enjoy a great weekend.

Best,
Nancy

Tiny Diamond

March 15, 2019

A Letter to Tom

The Ides of March

My dear Thomas,

Why do you suppose this date sticks in so many of our memories?

Actually, it is just another routine day here.

I am really happy that my Reiki Mentor, Sister M., has taken you under her wing and is training you to become a Reiki Master! She has great knowledge, considerable clinical practice, and a very holy aura about her!

I have a friend who comes over and helps me with chores. She is having hand surgery on March,17, 2019, for right hand tendon release.

Let's place her on our Reiki list, starting the evening before and for three more subsequent days, post-op. Using initials only in this book; hers are C.B.

I am keeping an eye on the homeless situation here in most of our major cities. These cities act as though they are unaware of the problem, and yet some small businesses are going out of business as homeless people are sleeping in tents, others right on the sidewalks in front of their doors.

Some cities have put in Porta-Potties and sent in people to clean up trash and needles from drugs, which are scattered all over!

A good man went there and chose just one guy. He took him out to eat, then to a barber to get a fresh shave and hair cut, then on to a clothing store for a new outfit, and on to a place he knew where his buddy was hiring. The man got the job. He has been made whole.

In the absence of responsible politicians who should be doing their jobs, is it up then to us to help one person at a time? What do you think?

In the spirit of Reiki,
Love, Peace, and every Blessing,
Nancy

March 20, 2019
A Letter from Tom

My dear Nancy,

I have been waiting to answer your last letter and to address your comments on the HOMELESS CRISIS, a problem which impacts our two worlds. I have a good idea as to what you are seeing there, and I can attest to the horror of the situation, from what the residents here tell me they went through. They felt unloved, and no one cared about them.

I am afraid our politicians will never "get it". These are human beings many who caught one bad break which seemed to reproduce and cascade, one after another. Mind you, there are some who want to help to make change and help these unfortunate people. They seem to know, "But for the grace of God, there go I." On the other hand, others say it is not our problem. Baloney! Just like money is raised for cancer, this problem is a cancer. Everybody needs to pull up their sleeves and help by doing whatever they can. Just buying someone a meal or cup of coffee, is a start. This whole thing must be dealt with one person at a time, not one system for all.

I get quite emotional about the subject. I am just too close to it here. And now I need to cool down!

I know you have kept the lights burning in more than one household until federal assistance, or something else, kicked in. You believe this could be eased by one family member looking out for another member of the same family.

We know there are few out there who are not impacted by an alcoholic or drug addict in their own families. And then, there is the veteran who dies serving his country leaving a wife and family behind, just a few missed mortgage payments away from eviction. A new law could deal with mortgage payoffs for these folks. There are so many ways to help. Let us keep a positive outlook as we search for ways to help.

Now, more about the Drive-In Movie Theater we discovered near our house. I put in your request for "Catch Me If You Can" with the manager, and he said, "Sure thing." The lady in the booth never charges us, just waves us through! We may miss some of the flick, but always enjoy going back next week. I find the cars interesting. We're in a 1957 Chevy roadster, and there are cars around us from the fifties through the 1980's.

Well that's all for now, my love.

Take care of yourself for me.

I love you so much,
Your Thomas

March 31, 2019
A Note from James
About Tiny Diamond

Dear Nancy,

I am here with a response from my father regarding Tiny Diamond.

James

Bob Murray's Message

Essentially, I received a visit from two dogs. They arrived at my front door in front of my house. One was a friendly dog named Rufus with whom I have had an acquaintance, before. Several dogs have visited me here over the past few years.

Anyway, Tiny Diamond was with Rufus, and I read the dogs' thoughts. Rufus introduced his friend. He literally gave me a picture of a tiny diamond in my mind, and I thought, "Yes, I was asked about this dog."

So we communicated back and forth. Tiny Diamond communicated that when he arrived here he was taken-in by some new friends, and He is now part of a pack.

Rufus said, "When dogs arrive here there is a serious need for immediate companionship. The 'Pack' helps them to adjust."

You would be surprised at the life many dogs endure on earth, but Tiny Diamond is a gem! Rufus meant no pun. Both dogs raised their paws in salute to say goodbye and were on their way back to their home.

Bob Murray

March 31, 2019
Tom Wrote
His Message to Nancy

My dear Nancy,

Yes, I have done some more regression work as Mr. Leopold. I put through the request for a tax-relief bill for the town of Galveston, taxes being a dry subject unless you have to pay them.

(James and I started this letter yesterday, but due to interruptions, we are back today to finish up.)

I was fascinated with your telling of the Reiki angel with Aids story, of how you received a phone call on a busy Saturday when you had much to do, but you took the call anyway. He asked you to give him an Rx. He was dropped off by the bus driver at a motel and gave you the address.

Your friend Cindy and her family were arriving for the weekend, so after dinner you said, "We have to make a Reiki call."

I am just surprised her husband or your mom did not object. You indicated you grabbed some Cokes and chocolate candy bars and were on your way. Most interesting was how no one seemed to notice you two walking in or going down the hall. His door was partially open, and he said, "Come in." Neither of you girls seemed to bat an eye when you discovered a very tall, thin man with long, black hair, dressed all in black, lying down on the bed. And the big trunk sitting in the room must have been a prop as in his condition he could never have lifted it. He was downright happy to drink a Coke and eat some candy.

Angels I have met here seem to love these treats we had when on Earth. As you began his Rx, you obviously were inspired to use the figure eight symbol on its side, i.e. the circle of infinity. I was also surprised to hear that you and your friend never discussed this strange event until years later. He said he was leaving in the morning, travelling home, and that was that. You never heard from him again.

You know what I think? I think it was a test! He wanted to see if you would follow the heart of a healer despite possible danger.

Thank you, my dear, for sharing that Reiki encounter. That kind of sharing is so helpful to me.

James seems to be falling asleep at his computer, so I will sign off for now.

Sending you a room full of spring flowers to light up your day and remind you how much I love you.

Your Tom

April 2, 2019
A Letter from Nancy

Good morning, dear Tom,

The encounter with the angel I described is one Cindy and I discuss from time to time.

It was all so staged! No one was at the front desk of the motel when we entered or when we left.

Talk about surreal! When inspired, we both raised up our hands over the man and began drawing the figure eight palm to palm.

It seemed, back at the time, we were not to speak of it either. Oh, I had a name and a fake address which he gave me from California.

I tried writing to him, and my letter was returned marked "person unknown." Once a healer starts down the path, we must always be ready to accept assignment, and as you would say, "Go with the flow."

To do any different would be like Jesus turning His back on a leper. It would never happen!

We are having a lot of rain here, and I can see tulips breaking ground. Before long, these Holland bulbs will explode, ushering in Spring.

It is the kind of day Gordon Lightfoot sings about in "Rainy Day People". In this haunting melody, he describes rainy-day lovers shedding a tear or two. You always seem to know when I am feeling blue. That is one of the things I love about you: your understanding.

I sent you another picture. It is the last picture taken before your departure. You will recall the lovely Christmas Day annual party held at Mike and Peggy's house. I remember throwing up my hand for Mike to notice us, and he got a great candid shot.

Our last move to the suburbs turned out great, having your brother Pete and Kathy and their three kids almost next door. You never missed one of their kids' games. Being a high school basketball star, Ki-Ki Calumet brought the entire team to your funeral mass. They made quite the entrance all wearing their red and white colors! At Communion time, I heard Shane whisper to Packy (our nephews), "I can't go up there; I have not made my first communion yet!" In typical Packy fashion, Packy said, "That's okay; just follow me!"

I wonder if you were present. I have heard some souls stick around for their funerals.

My darling I will close for now.

Sending all my love,
Nancy

HEAVEN-SENT LOVE LETTERS by Nancy S. Calumet

April 10, 2019
A Letter from Tom

My dear Nancy,

Yes, I came to my own funeral. I find, in talking to folks here, this is pretty common. It is a very confusing time for us, too. I wanted to be in the conversations, yet no one could see or hear me!

I am going to be with you at your doctors' appointment this week. I don't know exactly how I will do it, but I will ask Bob; he will know.

> (Nancy steps in: "I was sitting in an exam room in a wheelchair waiting for the doctor to come back in when the door to the room suddenly flew wide open. I saw the doctor and nurses at the desk but no one else; however, I knew Tom had arrived!")

Tom continues: When I checked with Bob, he said he would accompany me and come back when I was ready to return home. So I was there, my dear, even accompanied you to the lab. I am glad the acute phase is subsiding and feel the new medications will have you walking about once again. In the meantime, some of us here will be sending healing treatments to you until you are fully recovered.

Nancy, I love you more than anything and visualize you turning the corner and feeling better every day forward.

The dream you shared with me of a lovely lady visiting you and placing two pillows behind your head and shoulders was your soul taking care of your physical body during your sleep. You got the best sleep you had in days when you turned to your right side and smiled up at her before going back to sleep.

All my love,

Tom

April 16, 2019
Nancy Wrote to Tom

Good morning, dear Tom,

You once said my letters to you all come with your full name, i.e., Thomas Anthony Calumet, typed in the left-hand corner.

I have come up with an address for your house and mailbox: 2741 Heavenside Place. I got the numbers by combining the year you were born with my year. I took Heavenside from a poem I published. So it will look like this from now on:

Thomas Anthony Calumet

2741 Heavenside Place

Dear Tom,

I hope you like it!

Easter flew by, and I am happy to report I am feeling good and getting some early sunshine.

Caring is the golden rule for caregivers and healers. I feel like our working together; sending healing prayer; sharing the names, conditions, and progress reports between our two worlds is in every way a healing ministry.

[Ed. Note: For many years, Nancy has had a healing prayer ministry in which she receives requests for intercession on behalf of her friends and others, for special prayers. After Tom's training in her methods, they now gather a shared list of names and needs and pray together at agreed upon times. Thus, their prayer power is multiplied. While the power of prayer is widely recognized among people of faith, Nancy and Tom are unique in that their ministry spans across the Earth/Heaven barrier.]

And now a suggestion for you, Tom, is to explore what lies beyond your back fence. It sounds like a great adventure, and who knows what you may discover!

So you now have three children assigned to your care at the DR: Tommy, Ruth, and Abbie. How old are they?

I shall go now as it's getting late.

Moonlight hugs and kisses,
Nancy

April 22, 2019
A Letter to Nancy from Tom

My dear Nancy,

First, let me thank you for my new address. Honey, it's perfect. When I arrived home from work, there was a decorative plaque hanging on the porch by the entrance door saying "2741 Heavenside Place". Oh yes, it is on my mailbox, too, with my name.

Maybe you could suggest a name for the shelter. Just an idea. You're good at this.

I have been waiting to tell you about my little exploration beyond my back fence. I thought, "Nancy is right; I have no idea what may be back there."

So I started walking and seemed to be following a well-tread path through the woods until I came upon a large meadow filled with all kinds of wildflowers. I walked straight through till I came to an all-green forest. I noticed tall pine and other evergreen trees. Little animals came out to look and see who was walking in their woods!

Well, about twenty minutes later, I stepped into a little clearing, and there was a rustic cabin sitting there. It looked unoccupied. I went and tried the front door, but it was locked. I tried looking in the windows, but it was dark inside. I was unable to see anything. I thought, "I'd better go back home," and so I did. What do you think? Is it our getaway spot? That's the thought I received, and then I heard, "The key is on the mantel."

So I shall return later.

I will keep you posted.

HEAVEN-SENT LOVE LETTERS by Nancy S. Calumet

The work I do at the shelter is more mental than physical, but when I get to the Diaper Ranch, the kids keep me hopping. They are always under supervision and can be a handful. I think I mentioned, they assigned me three kids, whom they say are now mine. The youngest one, Tommy, is about five years old, and the girls are eight and nine. Ruth, the one with the beautiful brown eyes and wearing the pink hoodie, is the oldest and is very serious—so different from Abbie who has the blue eyes and long hair. The kids go to school year-around here and grow up much faster than on Earth. Of course, we give them days off and recess breaks.

Till next time, remember I love you and look forward to your next visit.

Yours,
Tom

May 2 2019
Nancy Wrote

Thomas Anthony Calumet
2741 Heavenside Place

My darling Tom,

How are you today, my dear? I can almost hear you say, "I am just fine."

I was happy to hear you received your new address sign to mark your house and the addition of your name and address on your mailbox.

I do have a suggestion for a name for the shelter. I can see a huge sign that says: WELCOME, TLC SHELTER.

See if Chuck, the manager, likes that idea. He is always so appreciative when I send treats for the residents' afternoon coffee break. I would be more than happy to send lunch on Saturdays. Let me know what he thinks of my offer.

I was thrilled to hear of your exploration of the woods, meadow etc., but most exciting to me was the cabin you found.

If the key is on your mantel, the cabin must belong to the occupant of your house, YOU! I can't wait to hear about your return trip and what is inside it, and I look forward to exploring with you!

How would you feel about publishing our love letters in a book? Oh, I realize they are personal to the two of us, but you have given me a glimpse of what Heaven is like, and to share this type of information may be helpful to other people.

HEAVEN-SENT LOVE LETTERS by Nancy S. Calumet

Prior to reading Bob's books and receiving your letters, I know I had no idea about day-to-day activities in Heaven.

Well, anyway, it's something to think about.

I had better close for today as I have an appointment for a pedicure this afternoon.

All my love,
Nancy.

May 10, 2020
Tom Wrote to Nancy

My dear Nancy,

It's always a great pleasure to receive a letter from you. I sit and read your letters, word for word, when I return home from work.

I sat down with my manager, Chuck, and gave him your suggestion for a name for the shelter. Oh, yes, he was all for you planning the Saturday luncheon menus and food delivery. We serve lunch to about one-hundred people including residents, staff, and guests. There are twenty kids in the group. We all appreciate your desire to help us feed the homeless. The folks sit at long tables and are served by the staff. We will furnish the beverages. If you would send me your menu on Thursday, I will see it gets posted on Friday. Plates, soup bowls utensils, etc., should all be disposable. By the way, we have twelve vegans.

When I got home from my trip to the cabin in the woods, I found the key in a pewter jar on the mantel. Key in hand, I made the trek back again the next day. When I entered the front door, the place had an unused, musty smell, and I opened some windows to air out the place.

The main room is quite large with a huge wood-burning fireplace across one wall. On either side of the mantel, there are two three-seater, brown-leather sofas with green and red throws and colorful assorted pillows. There are two rocking chairs facing the fireplace and a table for four with straight-backed, oak chairs beneath the window to the left. On the right side of the room is more comfortable seating, as well as a library and a chess set on a side table. There is a small, but adequate, kitchen, a bedroom with several dressers, and an indoor bathroom. And somehow, we have modern plumbing and electricity. It is strange, but the exit to the back porch is through the bedroom. All in all, it is well furnished and very comfy. How about we take off as soon as you arrive on Friday and spend the night? It will be a fun weekend getaway.

Nancy, I agree with you about publishing our love letters for the benefit of sharing what we have and all we have learned. If I had come across something like this prior to coming here, I know it would have helped in my adjustment. Waking up here was a shock to my system.

To be cared for by medical staff in an infirmary was not something I would have expected, but it is commonplace when you first arrive. When I was a boy, my grandparents were there for me, and so they met me in the infirmary and welcomed me to Heaven. Although my death seemed sudden and unexpected, according to the doctors, my cardio-pulmonary system was seriously impaired. Their eyes act like a CT scanner. The doctors see everything in the body, but they do lab work, too. After a few days of rest and recovery, our soul-bodies are perfect, with no illness or disease. I was told at any time I can change my age, so I opted to do that right away and selected my middle thirties.

Well, my dear, I will close for now as James has things he must do.

I love you dearly and am sending a big hug and kisses.

Your Tom

HEAVEN-SENT LOVE LETTERS by Nancy S. Calumet

May 17, 2019
Nancy Wrote to Tom

Thomas Anthony Calumet
2741 Heavenside Place

Hugs and kisses

Good morning, dear Tom,

I greet you this a.m. with a hug and a kiss!

I am so happy you explored our cabin in the woods, and I look forward to seeing it this weekend. Also, I'm glad someone thought to modernize the plumbing and provide lighting.

When ordering Saturday's luncheon, I made sure there will always be plenty of food to go around with more food to spare. I know you said some people are shy and are not attending yet. Perhaps you could place some box lunches out for those folks. What do you think?

Subs with turkey, ham, Swiss and American cheese, a bag of chips, and a brownie for dessert seem like a good place to start. Please check and find out who is delivering the food to the shelter. Oh, I almost forgot the vegans. Their boxes will be marked and will contain no meat.

I loved celebrating your birthday with just the two of us at home this year. It's still a very important date; and I'm glad we were together.

Why don't we each write an introduction for the book and ask James to do the foreword? I feel like we have plenty of time, but we'd best get started. How can it be you already have a copy of our book on your shelf? It appears that Heaven knows, even before we do, what we're going to do.

What is on the book cover, and how many pages does it have? I am not going to ask anything else, as you have already said it keeps changing.

I am writing to Dorothy to ask if she will be our book publisher. We worked together on my first book, and there is nobody better.

Well, sweetheart, I am going to close for today.

I keep you in my heart and send you all my love,
Nancy

May 30, 2019
Tom Wrote to Nancy

My darling Nancy,

I am glad James has made time for us today. We have some catching up to do.

Our getaway weekend was everything we planned for and more! We rode our bikes there, and we carried backpacks with necessities. Murial was there before us to get everything ready for our arrival.

When we arrived, the lights were on, and there was smoke coming from the chimney. Scented candles greeted us as we opened the front door, and the table was set for two. A fire was burning in the fireplace, and lamps were turned down low.

As we unpacked, we checked out the contents of the dresser drawers. There were all kinds of weekend clothing, and two long-sleeved nightshirts were laid out on the bed. They were not to your taste, so we just ignored them.

When we entered the kitchen, we found two plates of food ready for our dinner. We each had a steak, a baked potato, and a green salad with French bread. There was a note saying, "Dessert in the fridge."

When we sat down to eat, there was a bottle of red wine on the table. It was dark, full-bodied, and very much to our taste. We decided to have dessert later—much later.

We found our accommodations better than at a first-rate hotel.

HEAVEN-SENT LOVE LETTERS by Nancy S. Calumet

When we awakened the next morning, we could smell the scent of bacon coming from the small kitchen. By the time we got ready and entered the living area, our food was already on the table. We were served pancakes with warm maple syrup, bacon, and English muffins with blueberry jam. There was plenty of hot coffee, and when we were finished, we had time left to explore the outdoors.

There is a little creek running through the property, with a suspension bridge. And how about the great little fishing spot to be explored on another visit?

When it came time to leave for home, we were two very happy campers restored by our visit in nature at our own cozy retreat center.

My manager, Chuck, ran your suggestion to name the shelter "TLC Shelter" by the committee. They adopted the new name, and the sign is being made. Chuck thought you deserved to name it because of all the work you are doing for us with planning and ordering the weekend luncheons.

Everyone seems to love the meals you are sending. They asked if you would do them for Saturday and Sunday, too. The staff said there was no way they can compete.

I asked a friend, named Trevor, how the food was delivered, and he suggested we ask the kitchen staff. Apparently, two men arrive outside the kitchen's backdoor in a large, insulated truck which they unload. Afterwards they come back to pick up the refuse and food scraps. They take them to a local farmer who feeds his animals, and the trash is placed in an incinerator to be destroyed. It's like you say, Nancy, wishes are granted here, and in Heaven there is no waste. The truck-drivers said they receive a call to pick up and deliver the food. When they get to the plant, the food is there waiting, but they do not ever see any people around. Dubbed "Angel Chefs", they prefer to remain anonymous.

Now, the kitchen has to be enlarged. Chuck gave the staff a day off, so the engineers could complete this task.

Next, the dining room is scheduled to be made larger for all the folks who are now attending. A suggestion has been made for round tables with eight chairs. You are the one behind all this change. Chuck said, "Thank your friend, Nancy."

I said, "She is much more than a friend; Nancy is my wife!" He seemed surprised. Now everybody knows who you are, and we are a grateful bunch!

I have much more to write, but it will have to wait for another day.

All my love, hugs, and kisses
Your Tom

June 12, 2019
Nancy Wrote to Tom

Thomas Anthony Calumet
2741 Heavenside Place

My dearest Tom,

I really like the idea of the folks sitting around a round dining-room table. What a wonderful way to bring people together while breaking bread!

You probably know; I am still working on my Introduction, and I see you have finished yours. Good for you! It's great, by the way.

Marcia has signed on to do her artistic rendition of Murial, and Maddie, as she did for my first book, will do the cover drawing. My dear publisher, Dorothy, has graciously agreed to publish this book, too, and I look forward to working with her again!

I found a new movie to watch at the drive-In. From 1994, I bring you "The Shawshank Redemption," a prison film with a happy ending.

Thank you for placing P.J.P. on your healing list. His dear sister sent a picture of the cellulitis affecting his right eye, his ear, and going up into his scalp. Your effort was most helpful. When we have completed three days of healing work, I will send you a progress report.

I mention again the fact that your name and address font turns purple after I hit Send. Well, I had a new surprise: My closing and my name also turned purple on my last letter to you.

I think it is some sort of approval or loving hug from Spirit. What do you think?

So I will close for now.

Sending you all my love, hugs, and kisses,
Nancy

June 28. 2019
A Letter from Tom to Nancy

My dear Nancy,

Time seems to go by so fast. I haven't had a chance to send you my letter in a while, so let me make up for lost time.

You can let your friend and recent widow know I have located and spent some time with her dearly departed husband, J.G.

Once he left the infirmary, he was assigned to a pleasure tour boat and is happy to be on the water again. Since he was captain of his own boat, "The Snowy Owl," he is a lucky guy to have a job here so compatible with his Earth life.

I took him around town and gave him the tour, so to speak. We had coffee at a local coffee shop, and he left a tip. I explained we don't have to do that here, but he said he had this change in his pocket, which he didn't need. Do you remember I mentioned once before that there is no need for money here? That is one of the reasons it is so stress free. No bills arrive in the mail either.

You and I visit the cabin regularly, and the addition of comfortable, attractive furnishings showcases your decorating skills.

The engineers completed a hard-packed dirt road which skirts the meadow and leads directly to our cabin in case we want to drive there.

Of course, we could just teleport ourselves but driving or biking adds to the adventure. Am I right?

Our last movie showing was the light, comedic film, "Bandits!" I am looking forward to your next pick.

Films help bridge the gap for the past thirty years since I departed Earth, and I can see for myself some of the changes since leaving.

Now, for the color purple appearing in your letters to me: When I receive them, the areas you mention appear to be colored in a pale lavender. There is, also, a scent associated with every one of your love letters. Sometimes they smell like a field of wildflowers, other times like roses or gardenias. I am not sure what it means, but I will check with Bob and Murial to see what explanation they come up with. And with that, I will close for now.

All my love to my beautiful wife,
Your Tom

P.S. Can you imagine how stress free it is here with no bills to pay?

July 4, 2019...
Nancy Wrote to Tom

Thomas Anthony Calumet
2741 Heavenside Place

My darling Tom,

I am looking forward to news of the Fourth of July celebration party in my parents' backyard. I see your folks will be there along with some WWII vets with their wives. You asked me to send some type of food, and I am sending Kentucky Fried Chicken with all the sides. That is always good for a picnic.

I want to give you some feedback on our patient P.J.P. After only a couple days of sending healing prayer, yesterday he stated, "I felt so good today for the first time and was actually happy!" That is good feedback, eh?

I have varying comments with regard to black ink turning purple in your name and address. Like you said, no one knows for certain, but we all believe it denotes some kind of spiritual progress. I say that because when C.S. was typing up our letters she commented that, while she was typing, suddenly the ink color turned to purple on three successive letters, all of which had to do with spiritual progress.

I am so happy again since reuniting with you. It is a true gift—a veritable treasure—to communicate as we are. I can feel the strength and love you send me.

I thank God and His angels for bringing us together this way. If we have a secret ingredient, it is LOVE that holds us together! It never leaves us.

I keep you in my heart and send you all my love,
Nancy

A Note to Our Readers

Since this is the last of our letters to be published at this time in this book, let us take a moment to thank our friends for having read along as we have shared our lives and adventures with them.

If you, too, believe the impossible dream, try asking for what you want, and then practice the magic of believing.

All our love to our readers, friends, and our family,

Thomas and Nancy Calumet

GO CUBS!

Endnotes

And so, this portion of our book and adventure is now coming to an end.

We have taken you with us on our journey, and we have shared some of our more exciting happenings.

You have been with us at the library, the temple. the shelter, the cabin, the drive-in, the Diaper Ranch, and the infirmary; to name a few places.

Most importantly, you can see that a loving relationship never dies! Reunions and birthdays are still celebrated, and our deceased pets are waiting to be reunited with us if they were well-loved.

Whoever said, "The best things in life are free," said a mouthful, and it pertains to the afterlife. I know we have demonstrated that life goes on, and there is no death! You have learned that flowers bloom, gardens grow, entertainers still entertain, music is precious, and healing prayer is practiced. Nowhere have we encountered any soul misbehaving.

It does seem as though, if we have not mastered all of our lessons, we continue to grow and develop in Heaven as we would if still on the Earth. Souls are told to keep busy, and this seems to mean serving others. For that matter, anyone can do that right here on Earth in preparation for a life of service to come.

Whatever one wishes to learn can be studied there as well as here. Once I told Tom I wanted to learn to do the Tango, and I would like to have a beautiful voice and learn to sing. He replied, "All that is possible, and the best teachers are available to us."

When I leave this life, I expect to walk across that bridge straight into my husband's waiting arms! And so, as I believe, so shall it be!

Final Chapter

Now before we say goodbye to you, we wish to share with you the recent departure of a soul who is especially dear to Tom and me—my brother, James Clarence Spresser, PhD, (May 16, 1947 - April 3, 2020).

We are writing in real time when Covid 19 has swept the entire Earth in a pandemic, the likes of which we have never seen before.

Jim's death certificate says nothing about Covid. He died from complications of diabetes. When I received word he was hospitalized in critical condition, I immediately wrote Tom to watch for him and let our folks know.

At 7:30 p.m., April 3rd, when Jim was removed from the ventilator, he arrived at the infirmary in Heaven. Tom and my

HEAVEN-SENT LOVE LETTERS by Nancy S. Calumet

folks were there waiting while Jim remained in a deep sleep for the first three days. When he awakened, our mom and dad were just entering his room. The first thing he asked was, "Don't I know you two?" He was grinning! Naturally, there were some tears and a lot of hugging and kissing.

Tom went over and said, "Welcome home, big guy!"

When Jim got up, his vision was restored, and he could walk again. He asked the doctors about his healing and was told he had a brand-new body. The doctors wanted to keep him for a few more days as his passing was traumatic, and he needed time to recover.

When it was time for discharge, he went home with my mom and dad. I was kept informed by Tom and James as to what was happening.

Almost immediately, Jim said hello to me, his children, Shane and Amy, and his significant other, Anna.

An aunt who was caring for our dog, Coco Channel, brought her to the infirmary to greet Jim. He was delighted and said, "She remembers me!"

Jim wrote to me and told me about all the folks who welcomed him at a reunion party which was held at our folks' house. Jim said the first ones through the door were our maternal Grandma Irene and Grandpa Elzior, who took up chairs on either side of him as person after person filed by. He said all he had to do was just sit there and say hello.

Some folks seemed very interested in his teaching and directing of plays.

Almost from the beginning, he went to the library. Dad said Jim would come home every day with stacks of books to read.

Tom told me Jim was taking a course in molecular physics, and Tom asked him why that course. Jim said he had a new body now and wanted to learn everything about how it works.

89

Tom invites Jim over for pizza on Friday nights. They talk a lot about Reiki healing—something they both have in common.

Jim attends the Sunday luncheons at the shelter with the folks and can be seen riding a new red bicycle. My mom suggested Jim help serve, so he is doing that. Tom says Jim is making friends with some of the residents. Meanwhile, he has become quite well known at the library, and the administration has asked him to teach a college course in American Literature. He teaches in an auditorium, has about fifty students, and is busy planning curriculum again. A special plus are the guests—invited authors who now reside there. One might say Jim has had a smooth transition. Oh yes, he has his own new "digs", and he loves them.

Jim shared he never gave much thought to Heaven or what comes next. In that way, he is, possibly, like a lot of us.

It appears we now have some new information that may help us with our own transitions when they come.

If that is the case, we are very happy we took the time and effort to write this book.

In the Spirit of Reiki,
Love, Peace, and may God bless you,
Tom and Nancy

About the Author

Nancy S. Calumet is the founder of Tri-Angel Ancestry, a family partnership founded in 1992 for teaching Reiki and sending Reiki to those in need. She is a certified Reiki Master Teacher.

Nancy is recognized for her professional skills and accomplishments acquired over forty years in the nursing profession specializing in management, education, and quality assurance.

Widowed in 1990, it was through Reiki and writing poetry she found true emotional healing.

Now retired, she resides in Springfield, Illinois, and welcomes your comments. Her email address is:

nancycalumetrn@gmail.com

INDEX OF WORKS OF ART

(Used by permission)

Message in a Bottle, drawing by Maddie McAllister, page iii, cover
Murial, Original watercolor by Marcia McMahon, page xxi
Nancy's Flowers, Original watercolor by Marcia McMahon, page v
Five Tulips, Original watercolor by Marcia McMahon, page 64
White Flower, Original watercolor by Marcia McMahon, p.83
Child in Crib with Teddy Bear, by James Murray, page 51
Child with Teddy Bear, by James Murray, page 51
Flower Photos, by Sister Mary Ellen, pages 6 and 63
Cubs Game Photo by Nancy's friend Patricia Ann, page 85
Photos from Nancy's personal collection, pp. ii, 30, 39, 65
Photo by unknown author is licensed under CC BY-ND p. xix
Unknown Author is licensed under CC BY-SA pp. 14, 22, 31, 43
Unknown author is licensed under CC BY-ND p. 36
Unknown Author is licensed under CC BY-SA-NC pp. 4, 54, 56
Unknown Author is licensed under CC BY pp 31, 76
Unknown Author is licensed under CC BY-NC-ND pp. 7, 80
Numerous clip art pictures authorized by Creative Commons.

www.ingramcontent.com/pod-product-compliance
Lightning Source LLC
Chambersburg PA
CBHW042305150426
43197CB00001B/14